REFLECTIONS ON FAITH INSPIRED BY CHILDREN

Phil Ridden

EDWEST PUBLISHING

Copyright © Phil Ridden, 2020

Published 2020 by Edwest Publishing
Joondalup, Western Australia
www.edwestpublishing.biz

ISBN: Paperback 978-09925481-6-2

The author asserts his moral rights.
No part of this publication may be reproduced or transmitted, in any form or by any means without the permission of the author, except for fair use in worship and study.

To contact the author:
Phil@philridden.biz
www.philridden.biz

CONTENTS

Why this book?	vii
Why children?	viii
A word about Biblical quotes	ix
FUTURE	1
WONDER	2
MIRROR	4
CHANGING	6
UNIQUE	8
POETRY	10
MIMIC	11
WITH YOU	12
EYES	14
BEING THERE	16
SICKNESS	18
CRAZY LOVE	19
ASKING	20
HIDE AND SEEK	21
TANTRUM	22
WHEN I GROW UP	24
THINKING OF ME	26
HEART-SHAPED	28
DISCIPLINE	30
JUMPING	32
KISSES	34
PHOTO	35

KIDS	36
PLAYDOUGH	38
WHY?	40
RECHARGED	42
HALL OF MIRRORS	44
STARTING SCHOOL	46
STORIES	48
FAITH	50
ACROSS THE ROOM	52
PHOTO ALBUM	54
BEYOND UNDERSTANDING	56
WALKING TO SCHOOL	57
HOSPITAL	58
EXUBERANCE	60
MINI-ME	61
READING BOOKS	62
MOON	64
HOMEWORK	66
RETURNING HOME	68
STANDING FOR WHAT MATTERS	70
THE POOL	72
ADVENTUROUS	74
STUDYING	76
FRIENDS	78
BROKEN FRIENDSHIPS	80
WHAT THEY HAVE FOUND	81

ON HIS OWN	82
AMBITION	84
WAITING FOR EXAM RESULTS	86
GRADUATING	88
WORK	90
DRIVING	92
LEAVING HOME	94
HOME	96
FASHION	98
WILL	100
WE'RE GRANDPARENTS	102
FAMILY	104

Dedication

This book is dedicated to the children who have enriched my life, and to the congregations who have challenged me to share my understanding of faith.

Why this book?

More than fifty years ago, Michel Quoist wrote:

> If we knew how to listen to God, if we knew how to look around us, our whole life would become prayer. ... Words are only a means. However, the silent prayer which has moved beyond words must always spring from everyday life, for everyday life is the raw material of prayer.[1]

If we seek God, we will see Him revealed in the people and events in our lives.

Including children. The things they do and say and think and feel can challenge us to think about faith; reveal God to us; and teach us about our relationship with our Eternal Father/Mother.

That is the purpose of this book. As you read these reflections, it is likely they will conjure familiar images for you. I hope they will also help you to meditate on God and your relationship with Him.

This is not a book to be read from cover to cover. It is designed to be dipped into, sequentially or not, with favourite passages revisited from time to time. Perhaps it will inspire you to add your own reflections on the theme.

---

[1] Michel Quoist, *Prayers of life*, MH Gill and Sons Ltd, Dublin, 1963, p. 22.

Why children?

Children have always been part of our lives. My wife, Kylie, and I have four children and four grand-children, and for almost 25 years have been volunteer foster carers of infants. I was a teacher and school leader for more than 40 years and continue as a school board member; Kylie worked as a kindergarten teacher and, later, in child care.

We all have a responsibility to care for the children in our community. We all have an opportunity to shape the future through the children in our community. We all have an obligation to teach them hope and to introduce them to faith.

And Jesus reminded us that we have so much to learn about faith from children.

A word about Biblical quotes

A Biblical quote is included for each reflection—yet I do this with a little discomfort. It is too easy to extract verses from their context where they have a particular meaning, and to use them to convey another meaning in a different context. It is possible I have done that in this book—not to give credibility, but to help you to delve into the Bible and to seek out its truth. Forgive me if I've been simplistic. If the Biblical references are helpful, explore them; if not, ignore them.

Contemporary translations have been used. All are available (free of charge) online from various sites.

Bible Translations quoted:

Scripture quotations marked **NIV** are taken from *The Holy Bible: New International Version®*, NIV® Copyright © 1973, 1978, 1984, 2011 by Biblica, Inc.® Used by permission. All rights reserved worldwide.

Scripture quotations marked **GNT** are taken from *Good News Translation®* (Today's English Version, Second Edition), Copyright © 1992 American Bible Society. All rights reserved.

Scripture quotations marked **MSG** are taken from *The Message*. Copyright © 1993, 1994, 1995, 1996, 2000, 2001, 2002. Used by permission of NavPress Publishing Group.

Scripture quotations marked **TLB** are from *The Living Bible* copyright © 1971 by Tyndale House Foundation. Used by permission of Tyndale House Publishers Inc., Carol Stream, Illinois 60188. All rights reserved.

FUTURE

I imagine her in years to come, Father.

Sometimes I look at her face—
    the face of a child,
    innocent and wide-eyed,
And I imagine her ageing:
Her face morphed into that of an adult;
The passing decades shaping her features.
Just for a moment
I see the person she will become,
But then it is gone.

I wonder how you see me, Father.
Do you sometimes look at me
And see how I will change,
How the years will alter my features?
Do you see the person I will become?

Father, shape my life, my future,
So that I become the best of what you see in me.

For I know the plans I have for you, says the Lord. They are plans for good and not for evil, to give you a future and a hope. (Jeremiah 29: 11, TLB)

WONDER

I am overwhelmed, Father.

I cannot believe all she has learnt,
    done,
    achieved,
    become,
In just one year.

It's there
    in the photos,
    the journals,
    the memories,
    the stories;
Each great and small achievement.

I think my friends may be bored by my tales of
    her latest exploits,
    her latest triumphs.
But I cannot suppress my joy and wonder
At all she has done,
And all that she is.

Sometimes I'm overwhelmed by you, Father.
I cannot suppress my joy and wonder,
When I think of your great works,
All you have done,
And all you are.

*The world's a huge stockpile of God-wonders and God-thoughts. Nothing and no one comes close to you! I start talking about you, telling what I know, and quickly run out of words. Neither numbers nor words account for you.
(Psalm 40: 5, MSG)*

MIRROR

She loves the mirror, Father.

She stares at her tiny self,
    smiles,
    talks.
She has learnt that it is not another child,
But an image of herself.

The problem with mirrors is that
We see what we want to see.
Psychologists tell us that
Pathologically thin people
    sometimes see themselves as overweight.
Attractive people
    sometimes see themselves as ugly.
Narcissistic people
    sometimes see themselves as perfect.
We are not always as we see ourselves.

And we are not always as others see us.
Sometimes we try to be as others want us to be.
We try to fit the image that others have of us.

You are the only mirror we can trust.
You know us,
Not just for who we are,
But for who you created us to be.

Help her to see herself
As you see her.
Help me to see myself
As you see me.
Help us to find our best selves
In you.

But we Christians have no veil over our faces; we can be mirrors that brightly reflect the glory of the Lord. And as the Spirit of the Lord works within us, we become more and more like him. (2 Corinthians 3: 18, TLB)

CHANGING

She's no longer a baby, Father.

She's changed from a baby to a little girl.
It happened subtly.
Teeth changed her face;
Standing changed our view of her
 and her view of the world;
Walking changed her boundaries,
 and gave her liberty to explore more freely;
Child clothes replaced baby clothes;
Bulky nappies disappeared.

It's another phase in her growth.
It's another phase in how I see her.
It's another phase in how she sees herself.

Is this how you feel when you look at us, Father?
Do you see how we grow,
 not just in body, but in faith?
Do you look at us and see how we are maturing
 from babies to children to youth—
And am I yet an adult?

Am I growing, Father,
Maturing in faith?

I have had to feed you with milk and not with solid food because you couldn't digest anything stronger. And even now you still have to be fed on milk. For you are still only baby Christians, controlled by your own desires, not God's. (1 Corinthians 3: 2–3, TLB)

UNIQUE

I went to play group today, Father.

So many little ones there,
All the same—
    head, body, limbs,
    eyes, nose, mouth, ears,
    hair—well, some of them!
    fingers and toes, minutely-boned.

To an observer, just little children—
All the same.
Yet each is unique—
Each face recognisably different;
Each voice identifiably different;
Each expression characteristically different;
Each manner,
    response,
    personality,
Indisputably different.

Thank you, Father,
that you made each of us in your image,
All the same—
    head, body, limbs,
    eyes, nose, mouth, ears,
    hair—well, some of us!

Each wonderfully unique,
With our own personality,
    gifts,
    abilities,
    dreams.

Why did you make me the way I am?
Why did you enable me to grow the way I did?

Father, will you show me how to use my same-ness
    to connect with others?
Will you show me how to use my uniqueness
    to serve others,
And you.

For you created my inmost being; you knit me together in my mother's womb. I praise you because I am fearfully and wonderfully made; your works are wonderful, I know that full well. (Psalm 139: 13–14, NIV)

POETRY

'I want to cuddle you with my eyes,' she said, Father.

You heard her
    as she uttered words of love.
You saw her,
    as she held my face in her hands
    and in her gaze.

Did you smile like I did?
How does a child say something so profound?
Where does it come from—
This love that's unconditional;
This trust that doesn't question;
This dependence that has no fear?

Why don't I love you without expectation;
Why don't I trust you without question;
Why don't I depend on you without fear;
Even though you cuddle me with your eyes?

Keep me as the apple of your eye; hide me in the shadow of your wings. (Psalm 17:8, NIV)

Reflections on faith inspired by children   Phil Ridden

MIMIC

He mimicked me, Father.

I sneezed,
And he mimicked me—
    and laughed.

I know that he is learning so much
    from watching me,
And sometimes the responsibility is overwhelming.

What does he see in me
    that I do not want him to mimic?
Who am I
    that I do not want him to be?

Help me, Father,
    to be the best that you made me to be,
So that he, too,
    can be the best that you made him to be.

Remember your leaders, who spoke the word of God to you. Consider the outcome of their way of life and imitate their faith. (Hebrews 13:7, NIV)

WITH YOU

'I just want to be with you.'
That's what he said, Father.

I was busy doing what I thought important,
Shut away in my room.
And then unannounced, unexpected,
He was there beside me,
Squatting on the floor,
Running the toy car across the carpet.

'Why are you here?' I asked,
Resentful at the intrusion
    into my space,
    into my thoughts.
And he simply said,
'I just want to be with you.'

Guilt. That was my first feeling.
Tenderness, my second.
What did I do to be so blessed?
What did I do to deserve such love?
What did I do that he should want nothing more
    than to be with me—
Not expecting a story nor a game;
Just wanting to be with me.

Is that how you feel, Father?
I ask so much:
    do this for me;
    help that person;
    solve this problem;
    make that happen.
You must think me a demanding child.
How delighted you must be
    when I just want to be in your presence.

So here I am, Father—
    no agenda,
    no requests,
Just wanting to be with you.

Seek the Lord while he may be found; call on him while he is near. (Isaiah 55: 6, NIV)

EYES

He sleeps with his eyes open, Father.

At first we were surprised—
    even worried.
Then we laughed.
Now it is just part of him.

But it still surprises us sometimes,
When we look at him in the night,
    thinking him awake,
    then hearing his steady breathing
    and watching the rhythmic dance of his chest.

He is so full of life,
    so inquisitive'
    so observant,
    so aware.

We sometimes jest that he sleeps with his eyes open
    so as not to miss anything.
Nothing is going to slip past him,
No moment of life will be lost,
Nor anything to see unseen—
    even in sleep!
But you created sleep
    when we can turn off,
    when we can rest from life's stresses,
    when we can be at peace.
Do I sleep with my eyes open, Father?

There are times
When I am afraid to close my eyes—
    sometimes literally,
    at other times just wanting to be aware of
    everything.
Help me to trust,
    to believe that you will look after things.

I rely on your constant love; I will be glad, because you will rescue me. (Psalm 13: 5, GNT)

BEING THERE

He was just playing with other kids, Father.
    climbing,
    running,
    tumbling,
    rolling.
And then, for no apparent reason,
He sought one of us out,
Clasped a leg with his arms,
Looked up to check we had noticed,
Then ran off again.

A little while later,
    he did it again,
        and again.

What was that?
Did he want to be reassured that we were still there?
Did he want to remind us that he loved us?
Whatever the reason,
    it brought us joy too.

Are you and I like that, Father?
I know I'm preoccupied with my life
    most of the time.
You might even say that I ignore you
    most of the time.

But every now and then,
I return to your side,
Just seeking to be reassured by your presence,
Just wanting to let you know I love you.

I am always aware of the Lord's presence; he is near, and nothing can shake me. (Psalm 16: 8, GNT)

SICKNESS

Our child is ill, Father.

Not only ill,
   but suffering.
She hurts, she suffers,
   and I hurt and suffer too.
Every time I see her face contorted,
Every time I hear the sounds of agony,
Something rips at my insides.
If I could suffer for her,
   I would.

She clings to me for comfort,
And as I hold her,
I want to squeeze the hurt out.

Father, I do not need to squeeze:
I need only to pass your power through
   to quieten her,
   to comfort her,
   to heal her.
Fill her with your strength,
Your life.

At sunset, the people brought to Jesus all who had various kinds of sickness, and laying his hands on each one, he healed them. (Luke 4: 40, NIV)

CRAZY LOVE

I'm irrationally crazy about them, Father—
   my kids.

Sometimes they delight me,
Sometimes they disappoint me,
Yet I love them—irrationally.

I believe that you are irrationally crazy about me, Father.
I hope sometimes I delight you,
I'm sure sometimes I disappoint you,
Yet you love me—irrationally.
You call it grace.
Thank you.

This is love: not that we loved God, but that he loved us and sent his Son as an atoning sacrifice for our sins. (1 John 4: 10, NIV)

ASKING

She asks a lot of me, Father.

I told her: 'You ask a lot of me.'
She knew it was not a complaint—
 just a flippant observation.
But her answer took me by surprise:
'I do, and you always answer me.'

I do?
I do.
Not because I must, but
 because I want to,
 because I love her,
And she knows it.

I learnt it from you, Father.
I ask a lot of you—
 every day,
And you always respond.
Thank you for your patient love.

If you remain in me and my words remain in you, then you will ask for anything you wish, and you shall have it. (John 15: 7, GNT)

HIDE AND SEEK

You know about hide and seek, don't you Father?

He's hiding, I'm seeking.
I know where he is,
But it's important that I take some time
    to seem confused,
    to seem unsure,
    to seem unable to find him.

You know this game:
Jonah tried it,
But he learnt that
    we can never hide from you.

Perhaps sometimes I wish I could—
    when I feel I have let you down,
    when I am anxious about meeting your expectations,
    when I want to go my own way.
Perhaps.
But then I reflect on all you are to me,
And I am glad
    that I cannot hide,
    that in the moments when I most want to avoid you,
You find me.

Where could I go to escape from you? Where could I get away from your presence? (Psalm 139: 7, GNT)

TANTRUM

He had a tantrum, Father.

It was a ding-dong,
    screaming,
    rolling on the floor,
    kicking his legs,
    tantrum;
Precipitated by nothing much—
Just a decision by us to stay home,
When he wanted to go for a picnic.

His siblings were surprised
    at his outrageous behaviour.
They encouraged him to stop;
Offered to play with him;
Even offered him their favourite toys.

We took them from the room,
Leaving him without an audience.
It wasn't long before he realised
His performance was pointless,
    even embarrassing,
Having no impact on our decision.
We suggested he spend some time in his room,
Until he felt ready to apologise
And join the family activities.

It occurs to me that perhaps I
    have sometimes behaved that way.

When I asked you to heal my friend—
    but he was not cured,
    and I was upset with you.
When I asked you to help my child achieve her ambition—
    but she was thwarted
    and I was upset with you.
When I asked you to bring about change in my community—
    but nothing changed,
    and I was upset with you.

Father, I do not know your ways;
I cannot know your ways.
All I can do is to continue in the confidence
That you are active in the world—
    in my world.
I'm sorry if I rush on with my plans,
    then expect you to bless them.
I'm sorry if I decide your agenda,
    and am upset when it's not fulfilled.
You lead.
I'll follow.

I will lead my blind people by roads they have never travelled. I will turn their darkness into light and make rough country smooth before them. These are my promises, and I will keep them without fail. (Isaiah 42: 16, GNT)

WHEN I GROW UP

Don't you love those words, Father—
'When I grow up ...'?

I love to hear their dreams,
    their plans,
    their ambitions;
Sometimes expressed with hope,
And sometimes with absolute confidence
    that what they plan will be;
Some probably fanciful,
And others eminently achievable.

Some ambitions surprise me,
Revealing an aspect of their character
And their interests,
I had never noticed.

I tell them that when I grow up
I want to be an astronaut
And then a journalist.
They tell me I'm already grown up
    and laugh.
And I ask,
Is there nothing more for me?
Is there no future I can dream of?

Only you know their future, Father—
And mine.

Reflections on faith inspired by children   Phil Ridden

Yet, in years to come,
    whatever we find ourselves doing
    wherever we live,
    whatever we do,
I pray that we will find you there,
Leading us to the future you plan.

I'm writing as a father to you, my children. I love you and want you to grow up well, not spoiled. There are a lot of people around who can't wait to tell you what you've done wrong, but there aren't many fathers willing to take the time and effort to help you grow up. It was as Jesus helped me proclaim God's Message to you that I became your father. (1 Corinthians 4: 14–16, MSG)

THINKING OF ME

He was surprised we thought of him, Father.

When this grandson is not with us,
We think of
    things he would like to eat,
    activities he would like to do,
    places he would like to go,
    books he would like us to read to him,
    toys he would like to play with.

And when we hear he is coming to visit,
    we cook,
    we organise,
    we prepare.
Because we love him,
    his joy is our joy,
    his delight is our delight.

Is that how you feel about me, Father?
Do you prepare the way for me?
Do you plan things for my future?
Do you joy in my joy,
Delight in my delight?

You'll take delight in God, the Mighty One, and look to him joyfully, boldly. You'll pray to him and he'll listen; he'll help you do what you've promised. You'll decide what you want and it will happen; your life will be bathed in light. To those who feel low you'll say, 'Chin up! Be brave!' and God will save them. Yes, even the guilty will escape, escape through God's grace in your life. (Job 22: 26–30, MSG)

HEART-SHAPED

She wanted to know how to draw a heart, Father.

I'm no artist,
But I showed her the clichéd, stylised way
    to draw a heart.
It's what she wanted to know,
And she practised it
Until she was satisfied.
I then showed her how to form a heart
Using her fingers and thumbs.

I understand why we draw hearts that way,
But it is very stylised.
The simplistic two-dimensional shape
Belies the complexity of this fundamental structure.
The recognisable design
Conceals the nature of our hearts,
The values and beliefs
    that shape the core of our being.

I'm learning the shape of her heart, Father.
What shape is mine?
How would you draw it?
Is it shaped by you?
Is it shaped like you?
Is it shaped to enfold your people,
Your world?

A good person brings good out of the treasure of good things in his heart; a bad person brings bad out of his treasure of bad things. For the mouth speaks what the heart is full of. (Luke 6: 45, GNT)

DISCIPLINE

We've had to discipline him, Father.

You know what happened.
You watched us talk with him
And set in place some consequences.
He knew he had done wrong.
He anticipated the consequences.
He accepts—
Or seems to—
The discipline.

Of course, I've used the word discipline incorrectly.
Discipline is teaching,
    training,
    shaping.
We discipline him
Not just through loss of privileges,
But through example,
    discussion,
    problem-solving,
    responsibility,
    reward,
    and more …

But Father, as parents,
We are learning on the job,
And we won't know how well we have done
    until it's too late.

Are we shaping him in the right way?
Are we teaching him effectively?
Is he learning,
Is he growing
    as we want him to?

Father, you discipline me.
Am I learning,
Am I growing
    as you want me to?

My dear child, don't shrug off God's discipline, but don't be crushed by it either. It's the child he loves that he disciplines; the child he embraces, he also corrects. God is educating you; that's why you must never drop out. He's treating you as dear children. ... At the time, discipline isn't much fun. It always feels like it's going against the grain. Later, of course, it pays off handsomely, for it's the well-trained who find themselves mature in their relationship with God. (Hebrews 12: 5–6, 11, MSG)

JUMPING

She Jumped into my arms, Father.

She stood on the table
    and leapt into space at my call,
Knowing I would be there,
    trusting my arms to catch her,
    trusting my love to save her.

I remember when she became part of us,
    aged two:
Insecure;
Unable to walk properly;
Trusting nothing and no-one;
Fearful at being lifted up,
Or even lowered onto her back;
Terrified of any height.

But we taught her to trust our love.
Day by day,
Little by little,
She has learnt that we will not leave her,
    nor send her away.
She has learnt to trust our love.
Now she will leap from a table,
    trusting my arms.

Don't give up on me, Father.
I'm still learning to trust your love.

I'm still learning that you will always be there;
That I can step out in faith at your calling,
And your arms will catch me.
Teach me to trust your love.

Yes, because God's your refuge, the High God your very own home, evil can't get close to you, harm can't get through the door. He ordered his angels to guard you wherever you go. If you stumble, they'll catch you; their job is to keep you from falling. (Psalm 91: 9–11, MSG)

KISSES

She kissed me so gently, Father.

Holding my face in her hands
    as lightly as if I was a kitten;
She examined it,
    and then placed a kiss on the spot she had chosen.

We played a game:
When she kissed me,
    I pointed to another place on my face and said,
    'No, here';
And when she kissed that place,
    I pointed to another,
    then another,
    and another …
Until I was plastered in kisses.

Sometimes I think I demand too much of her love,
Yet she never complains.

Sometimes I think I demand too much of your love,
Father,
But I never hear you complain.
Thank you for loving me so much.

Praise the Lord. Give thanks to the Lord, for he is good; his love endures forever. (Psalm 106: 1, NIV)

PHOTO

I took her photo today, Father.

She loves to see images of herself,
So she was not camera shy—
    just open,
    joyful,
    authentic.
I think I have a true image of her,
    one that reflects not only her features,
    but her personality.

People say her looks,
    her expressions,
    her manner,
Are a reflection of me.

You made me in your image, Father.
But in the mental cameras of the people I meet
Do I project your image—
    openly,
    joyfully,
    authentically?

Help me to reflect your image in my life.

When God created mankind, he made them in the likeness of God. (Genesis 5: 1, NIV)

KIDS

Just watching them makes me feel tired, Father.

These kids
    run,
    trampoline,
    kick and throw and hit balls,
    swim.
They play
    with boundless energy
    and irrepressible enthusiasm.
They constantly seek new challenges,
    new discoveries,
    new experiences.

I sit and watch,
Joining in occasionally with a short burst of activity.
I am older,
But they make me feel tired.

Once I was a child in the faith, Father.
I sought you and served you
    with boundless energy
    and irrepressible enthusiasm.

I sought new challenges,
    new discoveries,
    new experiences,
    In faith.

Do I just sit and watch
Joining in occasionally with a short burst of activity?
I'm older now,
But am I also tired?

Help me, Father, to not use age
    as an excuse for reticence.
I want to serve you with energy and enthusiasm—
Always.

Even those who are young grow weak; young people can fall exhausted. But those who trust in the Lord for help will find their strength renewed. They will rise on wings like eagles; they will run and not get weary; they will walk and not grow weak. (Isaiah 40: 30-31, GNT)

PLAYDOUGH

They enjoy the playdough, Father.

It's a perennial favourite.
The feel of the dough,
    soft to the touch,
    malleable,
    yielding;
Warming with the play of fingers and hands,
    pummelling,
    twisting,
    sculpting,
    dividing and reconnecting,
Shaping it,
Until it takes the form they want:
    a dog,
    a burger,
    a person;
    Mummy, Daddy, me, fluffy—
        our family together.

The amorphous blob
Gradually morphing into a desired form
In the hands of the sculptor.

That's how we are with you, Father.
Our lives,
Lacking shape or purpose,
Gradually morph into the desired form

In your hands,
The hands of our creator.

The playdough does not resist,
But yields to the gentle power and influence
Of the sculptor,
Until it becomes what he wants it to be.

Do I resist you, Father?
Or do I yield to your gentle power and influence,
Allowing myself to be shaped by you
Into what you want me to be.

GOD, you are our Father. We're the clay and you're our potter: All of us are what you made us. (Isaiah 64: 8, MSG)

WHY?

There's that question again, Father:

Why?
Why are you having a shower?
Why is my baby brother inside your tummy?
Why did puppy wee on the floor?
Why are we going shopping?
Why can't we go to the moon?
Why do I have to get dressed?
Why doesn't my teddy talk?
Why is the sky blue?
Why are there stars?
Why is water wet?
Why is the world?

And just when I think I've won for now,
    the questions change:
When will Grandma come?
How does the picture get in the TV?
Who is boss of the world?
What will we do tomorrow?
Where did Grandpa go?
Some questions don't make sense.
Some things she is not ready to understand.

But I'm like that with you, aren't I?
I want to know why
    and when
    and how
    and who
    and what
    and where …
Some of my questions don't make sense.
Some things I am not ready to understand.

Like Job,
Help me to accept that
    there are things I cannot know,
    and things I may not know,
But I can be confident that you love me.

Why do you accuse God of never answering our complaints? Although God speaks again and again, no one pays attention to what he says. (Job 33: 13-14, GNT)

RECHARGED

His grandfather calls him a 'do-er', Father.

He plays,
    and runs,
    and laughs,
Seemingly without tiring;
Then, suddenly,
    he stops,
    and sleeps.
When he wakens,
He is re-charged:
    playing,
    running,
    laughing,
Seemingly without tiring,
Until the pattern repeats.

Such energy is to be admired,
Envied even,
But when it is spent,
He stops.

I've seen people like that with their faith, Father.
They serve you with energy,
    passion,
    commitment,
Seemingly without tiring.

Such energy is to be admired,
Envied even,
But when it is spent,
They stop.

But unlike my boy,
They do not always recharge.
Jesus told a story of seeds,
Some of which grow quickly in shallow soil,
But when the soil is exhausted,
They wither and die.

Am I like that, Father?
Do I serve you in bursts,
Carried along with enthusiasm for some new project,
Then wearing out and stopping—
Until the next burst of enthusiasm?

Make me a steady servant, Father,
Serving you consistently,
Beyond initial enthusiasm,
Beyond setbacks and struggles,
Persevering,
Until your work is done.

You are patient, you have suffered for my sake, and you have not given up. (Revelation 2: 3, GNT)

HALL OF MIRRORS

Everywhere we looked, Father,
There we were.

In this hall of mirrors,
Our images were
    in front of us,
    behind us,
    beside us,
    even above us.

And each image was slightly different,
Each revealing a different angle,
A different perspective.

You are with me in my hall of mirrors, Father.
In this life, everywhere I look,
There you are:
    in front of me,
    behind me,
    beside me.
In my present,
    standing with me.
In my future,
    leading me forward.
In my past,
    showing me lessons from experience.

And each image of you is a little different,
Each showing a different facet of who you are,
Each shaping my knowledge of you.

In the same way, we can see and understand only a little about God now, as if we were peering at his reflection in a poor mirror; but someday we are going to see him in his completeness, face-to-face. Now all that I know is hazy and blurred, but then I will see everything clearly, just as clearly as God sees into my heart right now. (1 Corinthians 13: 12, TLB)

STARTING SCHOOL

She's off to school, Father.

She was up at dawn
Dressed in her uniform,
Looking so grown up,
Yet so vulnerable.

How can I let her go?
How can I place this treasure
In the hands of strangers?
With your help,
We have gently shaped her into
The beautiful person she is.
Now others will shape her in ways I cannot know.

Is that how you feel about me, Father,
As you watch me achieve new milestones,
    enter new phases of life,
    take on new roles?
Do you worry about me,
And whether I will be able to withstand
The attraction of people and circumstances
That could corrupt me,
That might turn me from your way?

I know I will always remain in your love.
Help me to remain in your way.

Keep me from going the wrong way, and in your goodness teach me your law. (Psalm 119: 29, GNT)

STORIES

My children love a story, Father.

As I read, their minds are active:
Enjoying the sounds of the language;
Creating images from words;
Evaluating what is happening;
Anticipating the consequences;
Learning about the characters.
And when the time comes to stop,
Or when the story is complete,
There is often a cry of
'Don't stop';
'Just one more story';
'One more chapter, please ....'

You know how we love a story, Father—
Not just kids,
But adults too:
    stories told by good yarn-spinners;
    stories published in books;
    stories told in film;
    stories narrated in songs.

Is that why you told stories
When you were on earth?
Your stories connected with people:
    their work,
    their homes,

    their family and friends,
    their money,
    their comfort,
    Their distress …
And through the stories,
They learnt—
We still learn—
About you.

I'm not so skilled with stories, Father,
But I can tell your story,
The good news story of Jesus;
How he revealed your character,
How he opened a way for us to connect with you,
How he showed us how to live,
How he allowed us to begin again—
    for one time,
    and every day.
And I can tell our story,
The good news story of how we met,
And how we go on living
Together.

Help me to share the stories, Father.

All Jesus did that day was tell stories—a long storytelling afternoon. His storytelling fulfilled the prophecy: I will open my mouth and tell stories; I will bring out into the open things hidden since the world's first day. (Matthew 13: 34–35, MSG)

FAITH

I'm teaching them faith, Father,
But it's not easy.

At their age
They live in a black and white world,
A world where parents know all things,
    can do all things,
    can be trusted implicitly.
If I say something is true,
    then it is true;
If I say something is right,
    then it is right;
If I say I will do something,
    then they believe it will happen;
If I say I will help them,
    Then all will be well.

So I tell them essential truths about you:
You love each of them;
You will never leave them;
You will protect them;
You will watch over them.
And it is true—
But not as they understand it.
They will learn
    that life isn't always that simple.

Reflections on faith inspired by children   Phil Ridden

You love and care for everyone—
But when terrible things happen to good people,
> will they doubt your love?

You will watch over them and protect them—
But when they get sick or have an accident,
> will they lose faith in your presence?

Christians love other people like Jesus did—
But when Christians do unloving things,
> will they avoid the church?

If they ask for anything in Jesus' name, you will grant it—
But when their prayers are not answered as they expect,
> will they believe that faith is worthless?

How can I teach them faith
Beyond simple platitudes?
How can I help their faith to mature,
So that they are able to interpret all of life
> through the eyes of faith,

And so that they are able to interpret faith
> in the context of life?

Help me to model a faith which is constantly maturing
No matter what life presents to me.

Let us stop going over the same old ground again and again, always teaching those first lessons about Christ. Let us go on instead to other things and become mature in our understanding, as strong Christians ought to be. (Hebrews 6: 1, TLB)

ACROSS THE ROOM

He overflows with life and joy, Father.

In a new place,
It takes a few minutes for him to relax,
To feel comfortable with his surroundings,
    and these people;
But his energy cannot be suppressed.
Before long,
He is playing and laughing
With an exuberance that is irresistible.
But sometimes it overflows,
Overwhelming him,
Until he finds himself losing control.

We have an understanding.
Even across a room,
I need simply catch his eye,
And make a gesture—
Screwing the cap on the bottle
Before all the bubbles get out.
He smiles.
He understands.
He responds.

Am I ever like that with you, Father—
Living with an exuberance that is irresistible?

In Jesus,
You gave me life fulfilled,
    life abundant,
    life richer than I could have imagined.
Thank you, Father.
Help me
To let the bubbles out.

You provide delicious food for me in the presence of my enemies. You have welcomed me as your guest; blessings overflow! (Psalm 23: 5, TLB)

PHOTO ALBUM

We love looking at the photo album, Father.

Our children laugh at photos of us
    pre-marriage,
    pre children,
    pre-wrinkles!

They are in awe of 'ancient' fashions,
And the notion that these people,
    from a different age—
    or planet—
Could be the parents they know now.

But they also laugh at photos of themselves:
The toothless babies,
The falling, crawling, bawling infants
Who are themselves,
    from a different time.

So much changes, Father.
We look different,
We think differently,
We behave differently—
We are different!

And yet,
We are strangely the same.
We have each changed physically.

We have adapted to fashions,
    and to roles,
    and to changing expectations.
Yet we are still the same.
There is something
    in our features,
    in our expressions,
Which we know and recognise.

I love that you are like that, Father.
As I age, so does my relationship with you.
Yet you are still the same:
    the same in power,
    the same in wisdom,
    the same in knowledge,
    the same in love.

And I—
    created in your image—
Have I remained true to your image?

God spoke: 'Let us make human beings in our image, make them reflecting our nature so they can be responsible for the fish in the sea, the birds in the air, the cattle, and, yes, Earth itself, and every animal that moves on the face of Earth.' God created human beings; he created them godlike, reflecting God's nature. (Genesis 1: 26–27, MSG)

BEYOND UNDERSTANDING

She was too young to die, Father.

She was just a child;
Her life ahead of her,
Yet you let her die.

Why?
How could you need to take a child?
There are many who are aged,
    many who are unwell,
    many who are ready to go.
Why did you not take them?
Why a child?

You are a God of love—
Where is the love?
You are a God of compassion—
Where is the compassion?
You are a God of hope—
Where is the hope?

I do not know your ways, Father.
I cannot know your ways, Father.
Help me to simply trust your ways.

I know, Lord, that you are all-powerful; that you can do everything you want. You ask how I dare question your wisdom when I am so very ignorant. I talked about things I did not understand, about marvels too great for me to know. (Job 42: 2–3, GNT)

WALKING TO SCHOOL

She wants to walk to school, Father.

Her plan is to meet with friends at the corner,
So that they can walk to school
Together.
At her age, it's a reasonable request.
She can be trusted;
She won't detour;
She'll not cause trouble.

Yet I worry, Father.
She is out of our sight;
Left to her own devices;
Making her own decisions;
And so we worry.

Are we unduly protective, Father?
Do we worry unnecessarily?
When we cannot hold her hand,
We know you do.

Watch over her, Father, when we cannot.

The Lord will protect you from all danger; he will keep you safe. He will protect you as you come and go now and forever. (Psalm 121: 7–8, GNT)

HOSPITAL

He had to trust, Father.

He lay in a hospital bed in pain.
The doctor and I assured him
    that we would take the hurt away.
But he needed an intravenous drip.
He looked at the cannula,
It's long needle,
And he was afraid—
    afraid of what he did not know
    or understand.

We said,
'It may seem bad,
    but it will make you better.'
'It may hurt a little,
    but it will take away the hurt.'
'Trust us.'

He had no recourse,
    no argument,
    no power,
    no knowledge,
    no authority.
He had no choice but to trust.

I understood his apprehension, Father.

Yet I yearned for him
    to relax,
    to let my arms hold him and soothe him,
    to draw his strength from me,
And trust.

Do you often feel the same way, Father?
How often do you watch me, your child,
    hurting,
    suffering,
And yearn for me
    to relax,
    to let your arms hold me and soothe me,
    to draw my strength from you,
And trust.

When I hurt, Father,
Help me to trust you,
To relax in your everlasting arms,
Until you make my world right.

Whoever goes to the Lord for safety, whoever remains under the protection of the Almighty, can say to him, 'You are my defender and protector. You are my God; in you I trust.' He will keep you safe from all hidden dangers and from all deadly diseases. (Psalm 91: 1–3, GNT)

EXUBERANCE

I am amazed by his exuberance, Father.

Shall we play a game?
Yes! Yes! Yes!
Shall we weed the garden?
Yes! Yes! Yes!
Shall we clean out the shed?
Yes! Yes! Yes!
Shall we make some cakes?
Yes! Yes! Yes!
Shall we tidy the toybox?
Yes! Yes! Yes!

It seems that no matter what the task—
With a few exceptions—
He imbues the task with his energy,
Tackles it with exuberance.
I don't know if he loves to be doing,
Or whether he loves to be doing with me.

I want to serve you with such exuberance, Father.
Because I love to be doing,
And because I love to be doing with you,
And for you.

Love the Lord your God with all your heart and with all your soul and with all your strength. (Deuteronomy 6: 5, NIV)

MINI-ME

It's amazing how like us she is, Father.
I look at her and I see both of us
    in her body shape,
    in her facial features.
There is no doubt she has been made in our likeness.

But it's not just her physical characteristics:
I am continually amazed at her mannerisms,
    her expressions,
    her responses—
They are us too!
How can she be so like us at such a young age?
It makes me feel so proud.

I am reminded that I am made in your likeness, Father.
Do you see yourself in me?
Am I as much like you as I should be?
Do I make you feel proud?

When God created human beings, he made them like himself. (Genesis 5: 1, GNT)

READING BOOKS

She loves to read, Father.

Even before she could read,
She told the stories of her favourite books
    to her stuffed toys.
She loved to hear others read,
To share the stories with them.
And as she learnt to read for herself,
She read to her younger siblings,
Instilling in them, too,
The joy of reading,
And the delight of uncovering
The mystery hidden within the words of books.

And she loved to hear your word—
Especially the stories of Jesus:
Stories of his compassion,
    his teaching,
    his sacrifice,
    his resurrection,
    his love for humanity.

And as she matures,
She continues to explore your word,
To find deeper truths
That meet her needs now,
That answer her evolving questions about you,
That convey meaning and purpose to life.

Thank you, Father,
For giving us love letters
That we can read again and again,
To know
    and re-know
    and new-know
You.

Your word is a lamp to guide me and a light for my path.
(Psalm 119: 105, GNT)

MOON

We looked at the moon together, Father.

It shone so brightly.
Silver paint glistened on
    leaves in the tree,
    the edge of a branch,
    windows,
    gutters,
    cars.
It lay a streamer of light across the water,
    shimmering,
    shining.
'How beautiful is the moon,' we said.

No it's not!
Humans have been there.
They have walked its surface,
And brought back samples of rocks and dust.

We have seen that
    it is not beautiful.
It is dusty and grey,
With not a colourful plant,
    nor a moving creature,
    to break the monotony.
It is pock-marked with craters,
Craters within craters,
Blasted by meteors crashing to the surface.

It is not beautiful in its own right.
The glowing beauty in which we delight
    is reflected light—
The glorious brilliance of the sun;
So bright that it is able to reflect beauty
    from a dull, grey surface.

We say, how beautiful is the moon.
We should say,
How beautiful is the sun;
How amazing in its brilliance,
That it can make a dull moon
    shine in beauty.

Father, I am a moon.
Of myself, I am dull,
A thing of no great attraction.
Yet when I reflect your light,
    your love,
    your glory,
I like to think that I shine.

Do I reflect your light?
Do I shine for you?

So watch out that the sunshine isn't blotted out. If you are filled with light within, with no dark corners, then your face will be radiant too, as though a floodlight is beamed upon you. (Luke 11: 35–36, TLB)

Phil Ridden   *Reflections on faith inspired by children*

HOMEWORK

Homework fills his evenings, Father.

He is committed to learning:
To knowing all he can
About what he is being taught.

He is inquisitive:
Wanting to know about things not in the curriculum,
But prompted by his lessons.

He is determined to achieve:
Not to impress others,
But to meet his expectations of himself.

He is resolved to succeed:
To make the most of the opportunities
Which he has been given.

I admire his commitment.
He could achieve passing grades
    with much less effort.
He could be content with learning just enough
    to get him by.
He could 'wing it' in class
    adequately.
But no.
He wants to do the best he can,
To be the best he can.

Do you want me to do homework, Father?
Do I need to know more about you—
   to spend more time studying your word;
   to read and ponder about how it applies to my life?

I 'wing it' day by day
Adequately—
But is that enough
   for me,
   for you?

I delight in following your commands more than in having great wealth. I study your instructions; I examine your teachings. I take pleasure in your laws; your commands I will not forget. (Psalm 119: 14–16, GNT)

RETURNING HOME

I read about another one, Father.

Another child who had run away,
Who didn't want to live at home—
Not because of abuse,
But simply because her parents set standards
 she didn't want to meet.

But they sought her relentlessly:
 through media,
 through social media,
 through friends,
Until they found her.

There were no recriminations,
 no punishment,
 no angry tirade.
They simply wrapped her in their arms and wept—
 wept because she was safe,
 wept because she was back in their care,
 wept because they had missed her,
 wept because she was home again.

You're like that with us, Father.
Because we are your children
You seek us
Until you find us,
Until we are home again
In your loving arms.

So he got up and started back to his father. He was still a long way from home when his father saw him; his heart was filled with pity, and he ran, threw his arms around his son, and kissed him. (Luke 15: 20, GNT)

STANDING FOR WHAT MATTERS

She is aware of people with disabilities, Father.

There are many in our community
    whose bodies are not complete
    or fail to function efficiently,
And she notices them:
    those unable to walk or even stand alone;
    those with arms unable to reach for things themselves.
    those who are sight-impaired and need guidance;
    those who struggle to hear and understand conversation;
    those whose hearts and lungs and bodies are weak.

She is lucky to be healthy and whole, Father.
Give her legs
    that stand for what is right.
Give her arms
    that reach out to others.
Give her eyes
    that see suffering and pain.
Give her ears
    that hear the cries of others.
Give her a heart
    that serves others.

'When did we ever see you hungry and feed you, thirsty and give you a drink? And when did we ever see you sick or in prison and come to you?' Then the King will say, 'I'm telling the solemn truth: Whenever you did one of these things to someone overlooked or ignored, that was me—you did it to me. (Matthew 25: 40, MSG)

THE POOL

She swims better than I do, Father.

I flounder,
    flap,
    pant,
As I strive to make headway.
But this child,
    glides,
    effortlessly cruises through the water.
I sometimes envy her.

I sometimes envy her faith, too, Father.
I struggle
    and flap
    and argue
    and question.
I am yours,
But I always want to know more,
To understand more,
To do better.

But this child
    relaxes,
    breathes,
    allows,
    accepts,
    responds.

She too is yours,
But she doesn't need to know more,
To understand more,
To do better.

How can I relax, Father,
Trust you more,
Without always wanting more?

This is what I have asked of God for you: that you will be encouraged and knit together by strong ties of love, and that you will have the rich experience of knowing Christ with real certainty and clear understanding. (Colossians 2: 2, TLB)

ADVENTUROUS

I love his adventurous spirit, Father.

He couldn't wait to walk,
    and then to run.
To throw a ball and kick it,
    and then to catch it.
To climb on boxes,
    and then chairs and tables and trees.
To run,
    and then to jump and hop and leap.
To float in the pool,
    and then to swim multiple strokes,
To dive,
    from higher and higher boards
    in increasingly spectacular ways.

I am in awe.
He knows uncertainty, anxiety, fear,
But he puts them aside
As he confronts his next challenge.
He doesn't do it to win a prize,
Nor to impress anyone—
It's just who he is,
Always wanting to conquer the next challenge.

Sometimes I think faith is like that:
I reach some understanding,
Some moment of insight,
Some point of confidence,
And then I am challenged by something new—
A passage of the Bible I had never seen;
A question that I had never considered;
A situation I had never confronted;
An opportunity I had never faced.

It would be tempting to retreat into a secure place,
Where my faith is routine and comfortable;
But you challenge me to grow,
    to mature,
    to achieve new understanding and insight,
    to live differently.
Make me adventurous in growing my faith.

Consider it a sheer gift, friends, when tests and challenges come at you from all sides. You know that under pressure, your faith-life is forced into the open and shows its true colours. So don't try to get out of anything prematurely. Let it do its work so you become mature and well-developed, not deficient in any way. (James 1: 2–4, MSG)

STUDYING

They spend so much time studying, Father.

They revisit lessons to reinforce their learning.
They complete activities to test their knowledge.
They explore concepts to develop deeper understanding.
They write assignments to understand the applications.

These years of study
    at school and at home
Are important.
They equip them for further study,
    further learning.
But eventually,
The study stops,
And the application begins for real—
Not set exercises,
But open-ended tasks.

I've spent time studying your word, Father.
I've listened,
    and read,
    and discussed,
    and contemplated
Your teachings,
And your actions,

In order to learn,
> to test my knowledge,
> to develop deeper understandings,
> to understand their application.

But faith is for living,
Day by day,
Moment by moment—
Beyond set exercises.
Following you means living my faith,
In unpredictable,
> challenging
> unpractised
Circumstances.

Make me a student, Father,
Who is able to apply your word.

My counsel for you is simple and straightforward: Just go ahead with what you've been given. You received Christ Jesus, the Master; now live him. You're deeply rooted in him. You're well constructed upon him. You know your way around the faith. Now do what you've been taught. School's out; quit studying the subject and start living it! And let your living spill over into thanksgiving. (Colossians 2: 6–7, MSG)

FRIENDS

I've met her friends, Father.

There are two who love her for herself.
There are others who seem to be more focused on themselves,
Developing friendships for their own purposes.

Can she understand real friendship?
Can she recognise friendship which is manipulative,
    increasing status,
    inciting jealousy,
    seeking selfish ends?

Can she understand real compassion?
Can she recognise compassion which is false,
    wanting to be acknowledged,
    wanting praise,
    wanting to enhance one's image?

Can she understand real service?
Can she recognise service which is designed
    to impress,
    to win commendation,
    to affirm the ego?

Can she understand friendship, compassion, service—
And more—
Which seeks the best for others,
And not for one's self?
Can she discern it?
Can she live it?

Jesus is our example, Father.
A life of selflessness
That sought only the good of others
At great cost to himself.
Can she live that way?

Can I?

Since you have been chosen by God who has given you this new kind of life, and because of his deep love and concern for you, you should practice tender-hearted mercy and kindness to others. Don't worry about making a good impression on them, but be ready to suffer quietly and patiently. (Colossians 3: 12, TLB)

BROKEN FRIENDSHIPS

She has friendship problems, Father.

For no apparent reason,
Her friendship group has realigned.
Relationships have fractured,
And she is hurt—
Hurt because trust is damaged,
Hurt because relationships have changed,
Hurt because she does not understand what she has done.

She will survive, Father.
She is strong,
And we will help her to negotiate her way
Through ever changing relationships.

Thank you that your friendship never changes,
That you are reliable,
    trustworthy,
    unchanging,
In your love for us.

Friends come and friends go, but a true friend sticks by you like family. (Proverbs 18: 24, MSG)

WHAT THEY HAVE FOUND

They are well-schooled, Father.

They have attended schools
    with strong academic programs,
    and authentic relationships,
    and clear values.

They have achieved as well as they were able.
They are competent communicators,
Able to relate to people of different backgrounds,
And with sound values to guide their lives.
And they have learnt of you,
Recognised your influence in the world,
Understood your claim upon their lives.

Will they hold onto what they have found?

You are to follow only God, your God, hold him in deep reverence, keep his commandments, listen obediently to what he says, serve him–hold on to him for dear life! (Deuteronomy 13: 4, MSG)

ON HIS OWN

He's out on his own again, Father.

I know where he is going,
 but not where he will end up.
I know who he is meeting,
 but not who he will be with.

I know we cannot keep him under our wing forever.
He must learn to fly,
And to fly alone.

Is that how you felt about me, Father,
When I first stepped out from the protection of my family,
And the shelter of my church family,
To make my own way;
To take myself to where I wanted to be—
 for the next moment,
 for the day,
 or for life?

I knew you were with me, Father.
I knew you were watching,

I knew you were guiding
    my steps,
    my decisions,
    my relationships,
    my life,
Because I placed them in your hands,
And you will always guide me.

Guide me down the road of your commandments; I love traveling this freeway! (Psalm 119: 35, MSG)

AMBITION

I love to hear his ambitions, Father.

Like most young people,
He has plans—
    the career he will have,
    the car he will drive,
    the home he will build,
    the family he will have,
    the sport he will play,
    the travel he will enjoy …
Or so he plans,
    dreams,
    hopes.

And where do you fit in, Father?
What are his plans to give all this meaning,
    to find purpose,
    to serve you?

I remember my plans, Father.
Some were achieved
Beyond my imaginings.
Some fell by the wayside,
Replaced by better dreams,
Or perhaps more realistic plans.

You gave my plans meaning,
I found purpose—
I still find purpose—
In serving you.

Have I pleased you, Father,
With my dreams,
    my achievements,
    my service?

So now Israel, what do you think God expects from you? Just this: Live in his presence in holy reverence, follow the road he sets out for you, love him, serve God, your God, with everything you have in you, obey the commandments and regulations of God that I'm commanding you today—live a good life. (Deuteronomy 10: 12–13, MSG)

WAITING FOR EXAM RESULTS

The mood is tense, Father.

This business of waiting for exam results is stressful—
Not just for him,
But for the whole family.
We all feel his anxiety.
We all endure his irritability.

And yet ...
Sometimes I think we make too much of it.
These exams may shape his future,
But they are not the only factor.
Failure—or poorer results than he hoped for—
Will not bring about the end of the world,
    or even *his* world.
His life will not cease at this time.
His future will not be destroyed.
There may be some adjustments to his plans,
    some re-thinking of his course of study,
    some re-directing of his career path;
But life will go on.
He will succeed,
He will make a life for himself,
Irrespective of these results.

I know, because I've been there.
I've known failure,
    grasped from the jaws of success.

I've known confusion,
    thrown in the face of assurance.
I've known uncertainty,
    devouring plans created with certainty.
You were with me then.
We talked a lot.
I know you listened to me,
And I tried to hear you,
And to understand what plans you had for me.

Did I hear you right?
Did I understand your plans?
Did I follow faithfully?
Did I achieve the future
    that you saw for me,
The possibilities
    that you created in me?

Whatever the outcome of these exams, Father,
Be patient with him,
And help him to understand
That you know all about him,
Have plans for him,
And will never leave him.

We may make our plans, but God has the last word. ... You may make your plans, but God directs your actions. (Proverbs 16: 1, 9, GNT)

GRADUATING

It's the end of an era, Father.

No longer a school-girl,
No longer a child.
She has graduated ,
Not just from an institution,
But from childhood.
She has run the course,
    completed the studies,
    achieved the goals.

But it is not the end of learning.
Whether she knows it or not,
She will continue learning—
Not just from books,
But from life.

I know about learning—
I've been learning from books all my life;
I've been learning on the job all my working life;
I've been learning from life all my life.
I know it is sometimes exciting and stimulating;
But sometimes difficult;
    sometimes tiring;
    sometimes stressful.

Yet I want to keep learning, Father—
About you,
    and me,
        and us.
About faith,
    and commitment,
        and service.

Make me a learner, Father,
Always.

Are you tired? Worn out? Burned out on religion? Come to me. Get away with me and you'll recover your life. I'll show you how to take a real rest. Walk with me and work with me—watch how I do it. Learn the unforced rhythms of grace. I won't lay anything heavy or ill-fitting on you. Keep company with me and you'll learn to live freely and lightly. (Matthew 11: 28–30, MSG)

WORK

He has a job, Father.

My son,
Who I thought would never mature,
Has a job.

What he sees is
    remuneration.
What I see is
    regular routine,
    responsibility,
    requirements.

His employer will be less forgiving than his teachers,
    less accommodating,
    less willing to make allowances.
Work is not the same as school,
    or home.
He will need to grow up …
And he will.

He has been to school.
He has learnt what he needs to know
To equip him for employment
And the adult world.

He has the right skills,
    the right understandings,
    the right heart
To succeed—
Even thrive.

Is he also adequately faith-schooled, Father?
Has he learnt what he needs to know
To equip him to live out his faith
In an adult world?
Does he have the right skills,
    the right understandings,
    the right heart
To thrive?

Come to think of it, Father—
Do I?

My counsel for you is simple and straightforward: Just go ahead with what you've been given. You received Christ Jesus, the Master; now live him. You're deeply rooted in him. You're well constructed upon him. You know your way around the faith. Now do what you've been taught. School's out; quit studying the subject and start living it! And let your living spill over into thanksgiving. (Colossians 2: 6–7, MSG)

DRIVING

He has a license to drive, Father.

I'm proud—
    and terrified!
This is not a simple certificate of achievement.
He's of the right age;
He's been taught well;
He has shown himself to be responsible.
Yet there is risk,
Risks not necessarily of his making.
No matter how careful he may be,
    he can be distracted,
    the road can be slippery,
    unexpected obstacles can present,
    other drivers may lack control or concentration.
If he makes an error of judgement on the road—
    or someone else does—
It could change his life forever,
    or destroy it.

Yet it is part of his emerging maturity,
A tool to be used in adulthood.
I had to let him go
    when we first left him with a baby-sitter,
    when he went to school,
    when he slept over at a friend's house,
    when he went to camp,
    when he first went out alone,
    when he went rock-climbing …

The list is endless:
Moments in time when I was proud—
    and terrified—
Of his growing.

So I must let him drive.
I won't always be there,
But you will, Father.
When he was small
We played with toy cars together,
Driving them by placing our hands on the roof,
Controlling their speed and direction.
And steering them where we wanted them to go.
Father, place your hand on the roof of his car,
And guide the vehicle
When he is steering it into danger.

Place your hand on him,
And guide him
When his life
Is heading into danger.

The Lord will protect you from all danger; he will keep you safe. He will protect you as you come and go now and forever. (Psalm 121: 7–8, GNT)

LEAVING HOME

She's leaving home, Father.

Of course I knew this day would come,
When she would leave home
To make your own life in some distant place.
But it is hard for me to let her go.
I want to keep her with me for my own sake,
And because the father in me wants to think
She still needs me nearby.

I do not need to give her advice:
    she carries within her a lifetime's guidance.
I do not need to fear for her:
    she carries within her your Spirit to protect her.
I do not need to worry about how she will change:
    she carries within her the character of who she is.
She will make your own way in the world,
    and leave it the better for her passing.

But I will miss her,
And I will worry for her,
Simply because that's what a father does.

Is that how you feel, Father?
When I move into new phases in my life,
When I let go of familiar ties,
When I reach out to new challenges and opportunities,
Do you worry for me?

Please do.
I love that you love me
With a love that cares for me
Always—
No matter where I go,
No matter what I do,
No matter …

The Lord will keep you from all harm—he will watch over your life; the Lord will watch over your coming and going both now and forevermore. (Psalm 121: 7–8, NIV)

HOME

I'm glad they can always come home, Father.

They have left to make their own lives:
They will travel,
    find partners,
    accept jobs,
    establish careers,
    explore recreational activities,
    seek entertainment,
    nurture friendships,
    have children …
That's the way life is.

But along the way they will struggle:
They may have to deal with
    damaged relationships,
    impeded careers,
    illness and accidents,
    pain to those they love,
    unexpected setbacks …
That's the way life is.

And when they have much to celebrate,
    or pain to endure,
They know they can come home to family.

They will always be welcome,
    with a smile and hug,
    acceptance,
    encouragement,
    guidance,
    love.

I can always come home to your family too, Father.
The gathering of your people,
Who serve you
Wherever they are in the world.
There, I find
    a smile and hug,
    acceptance,
    encouragement,
    guidance,
    love.

Thank you for the family of Christ
That I can always come home to.
And thank you that I can always come home
    to you.
Will my children do that too?

Be gentle and ready to forgive; never hold grudges. Remember, the Lord forgave you, so you must forgive others. Most of all, let love guide your life, for then the whole church will stay together in perfect harmony. (Colossians 3: 13–14, TLB)

FASHION

They love fashion, Father.

The latest fashion is seen
    In their clothes,
    their hair,
    their make-up,
    their entertainment,
    their speech,
    even their food.
I guess that is how it's always been.
To some degree, I did it too—
Although my children cannot comprehend
    that my youthful attire
        could ever have been fashion!

But Father,
I worry, that fashion shapes
    their values,
    their attitudes,
    their understanding of right and wrong,
    the issues they choose to support,
    and the lives they choose to live.
I understand.
It is easy to be swept up in the thinking
Which dominates our media
    and our conversations.
It is difficult to stand against it,
    and to declare your truth.

Do I allow myself to be influenced
By the dominant messages
With which society envelopes me—
Even when they are contrary to your truth
And your teaching?

Don't become so well-adjusted to your culture that you fit into it without even thinking. Instead, fix your attention on God. You'll be changed from the inside out. Readily recognize what he wants from you, and quickly respond to it. Unlike the culture around you, always dragging you down to its level of immaturity, God brings the best out of you, develops well-formed maturity in you. (Romans 12: 2, MSG)

WILL

We've been writing our wills, Father.

When we have passed,
What we have now will pass to them.
We joke about
>the weird collection of mugs;
>the shelves full of books;
>my scribblings and musings—on pad and computer;
>the assortment of tools and fixings in the shed;
>the strange pieces retained from childhood,
>>or handed down from our parents;
>the poignant—often humorous—creations
>>which they made as little children for us—

Treasures of the past and of memory.

But there are also items of monetary value:
>collectibles;
>jewellery;
>special gifts celebrating milestones;
>a home and furniture;
>cars;
>investments and cash—

Treasures with financial value.

They will decide what to do with it all—
>what to keep,
>what to discard,
>what to liquidate,

what to gift to others.
They will decide what they consider treasure,
And what they consider trash.

Have we also left them, Father,
An awareness of your treasures—
    your love for us,
    your compassion,
    your wisdom,
    your word,
    your promises to us and all humanity,
    the joy of serving you …?

Have we acquired and retained the right treasures, Father?
Have we bequeathed to them
    the treasures we have found in you?
As they sift through the minutiae of our lives,
    will they also find these treasures?

And since we are his children, we will share his treasures — for all God gives to his Son Jesus is now ours too. (Romans 8: 17, TLB)

WE'RE GRANDPARENTS

We're grandparents, Father.

We're excited,
We're overwhelmed,
We're fascinated,
And we're apprehensive.

We're new to this role.
How must we behave?
How much attention is too much?
How much visiting is too often?
How many gifts are too extravagant?
How many photos are too many?
How many anecdotes of this little one's
    mannerisms,
    behaviours,
    achievements,
    milestones,
Are excessive?

We don't know.
We're not sure we care.
Our children
And our friends
    understand our joy,
And they will be patient—
    hopefully.

Thank you for grandchildren.
It's a new sort of love—
> not more,
> not less,
> just different.

I know you don't have grandchildren, Father.
You make us all your children.
And yet,
When your children
Introduce their children
To you,
Do you feel the pride of a grandparent too?

See what great love the Father has lavished on us, that we should be called children of God! And that is what we are! (1 John 3: 1, NIV)

FAMILY

I'm glad we have family, Father.

With family, we can be ourselves,
    free from the pressures to perform and conform.
With family, we are known,
    for who we are and how we choose to be.
With family, we are challenged to grow,
    to be the best we can be.
With family, we are taught
    by those whose lives are examples to us.
With family, we can share with honesty,
    and find honesty reciprocated.
With family, we can find support,
    in our most vulnerable moments.
With family, we are accepted,
    with no need to prove our worth.
With family, we have history,
    stories to share of those who have gone before us.
With family, we have a future,
    with people who will always be there.
With family, we are loved,
    unconditionally.
I'm glad that we have our family.

And I'm glad that we have your family, Father—
    the church.

With them, too, we can be ourselves,
> free from the pressures to perform and conform.

With them, we are known,
> for who we are and how we choose to be.

With them, we are challenged to grow,
> to be the best we can be.

With them, we are taught
> by those whose lives are examples to us.

With them, we can share with honesty,
> and find honesty reciprocated.

With them, we can find support,
> in our most vulnerable moments.

With them, we are accepted,
> with no need to prove our worth.

With them, we have history,
> stories to share of those who have gone before us.

With them, we have a future,
> with people who will always be there.

With them, we are loved,
> unconditionally.

I'm glad that we have your family, Father,
The family Jesus created,
The family he heads.

The church is Christ's body, in which he speaks and acts, by which he fills everything with his presence. (Ephesians 1: 23, MSG)

By the same author:

Reflections on faith inspired by seniors

Reflections on faith inspired by men

Reflections on faith inspired by babies

Reflections on faith inspired by COVID

Faith around the barbecue (The story)

Faith around the barbecue (The play)

Go to **www.philridden.biz**

www.ingramcontent.com/pod-product-compliance
Lightning Source LLC
Chambersburg PA
CBHW070433010526
44118CB00014B/2025